100 MIND-BLOWING MMA FACTS

100 Epic Stories from the Most Insane Fights in MMA History

FELIX GRAYSON

MINDSPARK PUBLISHING

Copyright © 2025 by MindSpark Publishing

All rights reserved. No part of this book may be reproduced, stored in a retrieval system, or transmitted in any form or by any means—electronic, mechanical, photocopying, recording, or otherwise—without the prior written permission of the publisher, except in the case of brief quotations embodied in critical articles or reviews.

This book is intended to provide general information on the topics discussed and is not intended as a substitute for professional advice. Every effort has been made to ensure accuracy, but the author and publisher assume no responsibility for errors, omissions, or contrary interpretation of the subject matter.

Published by MindSpark Publishing.
Cover design by MindSpark Publishing.

CONTENTS

Before We Dive In... 8

Introduction 10

The Fastest Knockout in UFC History 13

The Fighter Who Won with a Broken Arm 15

The Only UFC Fighter to Fight with One Arm 17

The Time a Fighter Won... While Unconscious 19

The Fighter Who Broke His Leg... Kicking 21

The Only Fighter to Hold Two UFC Titles... Twice! 23

The UFC Fighter Who Fought With a Torn ACL 25

The Fighter Who Won a UFC Title with One Eye 27

The Bloodiest Fight in UFC History 29

The Only Fighter to Win a UFC Title Without Throwing a Punch 31

The Fighter Who Got Knocked Out... Then Won Anyway 33

The Only UFC Fighter to Win a Fight by Slamming Himself 35

The Fighter Who Dislocated His Shoulder and Popped It Back In 37

The Only Fighter to Win a UFC Fight with a Toe Lock 39

The UFC Fighter Who Won with a Backflip Kick 41

The Fighter Who Broke His Opponent's Arm... But Lost the Fight 43

The Fastest Title Fight Knockout in UFC History 45

The Only UFC Fighter to Win a Fight with a Twister 47

The Fighter Who Kept Fighting with His Ear Hanging Off 49

The Only Fighter to Lose a UFC Fight by TKO... Due to Vomiting 51

The Only Fighter to Win a UFC Fight with a Spine-Bending Boston Crab .. 53

The Fighter Who Won a UFC Fight with a Broken Skull 55

The Only UFC Fighter to Win by TKO… Due to Leg Cramps 57

The Fighter Who Kept Fighting After Getting Choked Unconscious 59

The UFC Fighter Who Broke His Opponent's Jaw with One Punch 61

The Only UFC Fighter to Win by Knocking Himself Out 63

The UFC Fighter Who Fought with His Toes Hanging Off 65

The UFC Fighter Who Won a Fight… With a Dislocated Shoulder 67

The UFC Fighter Who Broke His Hand in Round 1… and Still Won 69

The Fighter Who Won a UFC Fight Without Throwing a Strike 71

The Only UFC Fighter to Win a Fight by Running Out the Clock 73

The Fighter Who Won a UFC Fight While Screaming in Pain 75

The Only UFC Fighter to Win a Fight with a Ninja Choke 77

The Fighter Who Won with a Broken Forearm 79

The Fighter Who Landed the Most Strikes in a Single UFC Fight 81

The UFC Fighter Who Won a Fight with a Collapsed Lung 83

The Fighter Who Won a UFC Fight with a Broken Jaw 85

The UFC Fighter Who Dislocated His Shoulder Celebrating a Win 87

Knocking Out His Opponent While Getting Knocked Out 89

The Only UFC Fighter to Win by Slamming an Opponent Unconscious 91

The UFC Fighter Who Won a Fight With a Broken Foot 93

The Fighter Who Won a UFC Fight With a Torn ACL 95

The Only UFC Fighter to Win a Fight by Punching the Body 97

The Only UFC Fighter to Win a Fight by Leg Kicks Alone 99

The UFC Fighter Who Dislocated His Shoulder Throwing a Punch 101

The Only UFC Fighter to Win a Fight After Losing a Tooth 103

The Only UFC Fight Stopped Due to Too Many Eye Pokes 105

The UFC Fighter Who Won After Breaking Both Hands 107

The Only UFC Fight Stopped Due to Vomiting 109

The Only UFC Fighter to Win a Fight While Missing a Finger 111

The Fastest Submission in UFC History 113

The Only UFC Fighter to Win After Being Knocked Out 115

The Only UFC Fighter to Win by TKO… Due to a Dislocated Shoulder ... 117

The Only UFC Fighter to Win a Fight With a Double Knockdown 119

The Fighter Who Won a UFC Fight With a Broken Neck 121

The Fighter Who Won a UFC Fight With a Collapsed Lung 123

The Only UFC Fighter to Win a Fight While Blind in One Eye 125

The UFC Fighter Who Won a Fight With His Jaw Wired Shut 127

The UFC Fighter Who Won a Fight With a Torn Bicep 129

The Only UFC Fighter to Win a Fight With a Broken Back 131

The UFC Fighter Who Won After Tearing His ACL in Round One 133

The Only UFC Fighter to Win a Fight After Breaking His Arm on a Kick . 135

The Fighter Who Won a UFC Fight With a Broken Foot 137

The Only UFC Fighter to Win a Fight With a Torn Hamstring 139

The Only UFC Fighter to Win a Fight With a Dislocated Rib 141

The Only UFC Fighter to Win After Getting His Nose Broken 143

The UFC Fighter Who Won a Fight With a Broken Orbital Bone 145

Winning a Fight With a Broken Hand and a Broken Foot 147

The Only UFC Fighter to Win After Being Dropped Five Times 149

The Only UFC Fighter to Win a Fight After Tearing Both ACLs 151

The Only UFC Fighter to Win a Fight After Dislocating His Elbow 153

The Only UFC Fighter to Win a Fight After Losing a Tooth Mid-Fight 155

The Fighter Who Won With a Dislocated Wrist 157

The Only UFC Fighter to Win a Fight After Being Choked Unconscious .. 159

The UFC Fighter Who Won a Fight While Bleeding from Both Eyes 161

The Only UFC Fighter to Win a Fight After Breaking His Shin 163

The Fighter Who Won a UFC Fight With a Completely Swollen Eye 165

The UFC Fighter Who Won a Fight With a Dislocated Finger 167

The Fighter Who Won a UFC Fight With a Broken Nose and Jaw 169

The Only Fighter to Win With a Completely Swollen Shut Eye 171

The Only UFC Fighter to Win a Fight While Vomiting Backstage 173

The Only Fighter to Win While Fighting Off a Staph Infection 175

The Only UFC Fighter to Win After Tearing His Achilles Mid-Fight 177

The Only UFC Fighter to Win a Fight With a Broken Collarbone 179

The Fighter Who Won With a Completely Swollen Shut Mouth 181

The Only Fighter to Win After Breaking His Nose in the First Punch 183

The Only UFC Fighter to Win After Fighting with a Broken Rib 185

The Fighter Who Won a UFC Fight With a Dislocated Thumb 187

The Fighter Who Won a UFC Fight With a Torn Rotator Cuff 189

The Only UFC Fighter to Win a Fight With a Torn Meniscus 191

The Fighter Who Won a UFC Fight With a Dislocated Hip 193

The Fighter Who Won a UFC Fight With a Fractured Spine 195

The Fighter Who Won a UFC Fight With a Broken Eye Socket 197

The Only UFC Fighter to Win After Getting Knocked Down Four Times . 199

The Only UFC Fighter to Win a Fight While Barely Able to Walk 201

The Fighter Who Won a UFC Fight With a Broken Ankle 203

The Fighter Who Won a UFC Fight With a Broken Forearm 205

The Fighter Who Won a UFC Fight After Losing a Pint of Blood 207

The Only Fighter to Win With a Completely Swollen Shut Eye 209

The Only UFC Fighter to Win a Fight With a Completely Broken Jaw 211
Conclusion 212
Acknowledgements 214
About the Author 216

BEFORE WE DIVE IN...

Did you know that this is just **one** of many **mind-blowing** books waiting to be discovered?

What if I told you there's a **world of jaw-dropping, unbelievable, and downright bizarre facts** across **sports, science, history, mysteries, and more**—each one packed with stories that will **challenge what you thought you knew?**

EVER WONDERED WHAT IT'S LIKE TO...

- Witness **record-breaking Olympic moments** that defy human limits?

- Explore **real-life conspiracy theories** that sound too wild to be true?

- Discover **unsolved mysteries** that still leave experts baffled?

- Learn about **billionaires, stock market**

crashes, and money secrets?

- Find out how **robots, AI, and space travel** are shaping the future?

- Experience the **most extreme sports, legendary battles, and shocking events?**

This is just the beginning. The **100 Mind-Blowing series** covers it **all**.

WANT TO SEE WHAT'S NEXT?

Go to **FelixGrayson.com** and explore the **growing collection** of books and audiobooks that will **entertain, amaze, and keep you coming back for more.**

Curiosity doesn't stop here—this is just the beginning. What will blow your mind next?

INTRODUCTION

Welcome to *100 Mind-Blowing MMA Facts*, a collection designed to make you say, **"Wait, that actually happened?"** From shocking knockouts to legendary comebacks, this book is packed with the wildest, weirdest, and most unbelievable moments in MMA history.

Have you ever heard of a fighter **winning a fight while unconscious**? Or how about someone **breaking their leg on a kick—but still trying to stand up**? What about the time a fighter **won a championship with just one working eye**? These are just a few of the jaw-dropping stories waiting for you inside.

Each fact has been carefully chosen to **shock, entertain, and give you a whole new appreciation for the sheer madness of MMA.** Whether you're a die-hard fan or just curious about the sport's craziest moments, this book has something for everyone.

So sit back, relax (or get hyped!), and get ready to relive **some of the most insane,** mind-blowing moments in MMA history. Let's dive in!

Mind-Blowing MMA Fact #1

MIND-BLOWING MMA FACT #1

THE FASTEST KNOCKOUT IN UFC HISTORY

Jorge Masvidal holds the record for the fastest knockout in UFC history—just **5 seconds**!

At UFC 239 in 2019, Masvidal faced off against Ben Askren in what was expected to be a grueling fight. But as soon as the fight started, Masvidal sprinted across the cage and delivered a devastating flying knee to Askren's head, knocking him out cold. The referee barely had time to react before the fight was over. Masvidal's KO was so fast that even replay footage barely captured the moment in real-time. It remains one of the most unforgettable moments in MMA history.

Mind-Blowing MMA Fact #2

MIND-BLOWING MMA FACT #2

THE FIGHTER WHO WON WITH A BROKEN ARM

Most fighters would quit with a broken arm—Not Frank Mir.

At UFC 48 in 2004, Frank Mir faced Tim Sylvia for the UFC Heavyweight Championship. Early in the first round, Mir locked Sylvia in a tight armbar, and in a split second—**SNAP!** Sylvia's arm broke, but he refused to tap! The referee had to step in and stop the fight, awarding Mir the victory. Even crazier? Sylvia still argued with officials, insisting he could keep fighting **despite his arm hanging limp.** The x-ray later showed a **clean break**. This remains one of the most gruesome yet legendary moments in MMA history.

Mind-Blowing MMA Fact #3

MIND-BLOWING MMA FACT #3

THE ONLY UFC FIGHTER TO FIGHT WITH ONE ARM

Nick Newell proved you don't need two arms to dominate in MMA.

Born with a congenital amputation, Nick Newell has only one fully developed arm—but that didn't stop him from becoming a **high-level MMA fighter.** Despite the odds, Newell racked up an impressive record, even earning a shot at a UFC contract. His **grappling was so elite** that he submitted multiple opponents with one-armed chokes! In 2018, he fought on Dana White's Contender Series, proving to the world that disability is no match for determination. Though he didn't win a UFC contract, he remains one of the most inspiring figures in MMA history.

Mind-Blowing MMA Fact #4

MIND-BLOWING MMA FACT #4

THE TIME A FIGHTER WON... WHILE UNCONSCIOUS

Matt Hughes technically won a fight **while knocked out!**

In 2001, UFC legend Matt Hughes faced Carlos Newton for the welterweight title. Newton locked in a tight **triangle choke**, and Hughes was in deep trouble. But just as Hughes **started to pass out**, he instinctively lifted Newton high into the air—and then collapsed! The problem? Newton was still in his grip and **smashed headfirst into the mat, knocking himself out.**

The referee checked both fighters and saw Hughes slowly waking up while Newton lay motionless. **Hughes, despite briefly losing consciousness, was declared the winner!** It remains one of the most bizarre finishes in MMA history.

Mind-Blowing MMA Fact #5

MIND-BLOWING MMA FACT #5

THE FIGHTER WHO BROKE HIS LEG… KICKING

Anderson Silva's leg **snapped in half** during a kick — one of MMA's most gruesome moments.

At UFC 168 in 2013, Anderson Silva was attempting to reclaim his middleweight title against Chris Weidman. In the second round, Silva threw a powerful leg kick — but Weidman **checked** it perfectly. The impact was so brutal that Silva's shin **snapped in half on contact.**

The worst part? Silva didn't immediately realize it. As he stepped back to plant his foot, his leg **folded under him** in a horrifying scene that left fans speechless. The injury put Silva out of action for over a year, marking one of the most shocking moments in UFC history.

Mind-Blowing MMA Fact #6

MIND-BLOWING MMA FACT #6

THE ONLY FIGHTER TO HOLD TWO UFC TITLES... TWICE!

Daniel Cormier made history by becoming the **first fighter to win two UFC belts twice.**

In 2018, Cormier shocked the world when he **knocked out Stipe Miocic** to win the UFC Heavyweight Championship—while already holding the Light Heavyweight title. This made him only the second "Champ-Champ" in UFC history. But what makes Cormier unique? **He's the only fighter to have won both belts again!**

After being stripped of the Light Heavyweight title, he later **reclaimed** the Heavyweight belt in a rematch against Miocic. This feat cements Cormier as one of the greatest fighters of all time—**a double champion, twice over.**

Mind-Blowing MMA Fact #7

MIND-BLOWING MMA FACT #7

THE UFC FIGHTER WHO FOUGHT WITH A TORN ACL

Most fighters pull out with an injury—Thiago Santos fought Jon Jones with **both knees destroyed!**

At UFC 239 in 2019, Thiago Santos challenged Jon Jones for the light heavyweight title. Early in the fight, Santos **tore his ACL, MCL, PCL, and meniscus in his left knee.** Most fighters would have quit—but not Santos. Incredibly, he kept fighting for **five full rounds,** relying on his striking and pure grit.

Even crazier? **One judge actually scored the fight in his favor!** Despite the injuries, Santos pushed Jones to one of the toughest decisions of his career. He later required **double knee surgery,** proving just how insane his toughness was.

Mind-Blowing MMA Fact #8

THE FIGHTER WHO WON A UFC TITLE WITH ONE EYE

Michael Bisping became **UFC champion—despite being blind in one eye!**

Bisping lost vision in his right eye after a brutal head kick from Vitor Belfort in 2013. The damage was so severe that doctors diagnosed him with a **detached retina**—but Bisping refused to retire. Instead, he **hid the injury** from the UFC for years, passing medical exams with tricks like covering his good eye in training to compensate.

In 2016, against all odds, Bisping **knocked out Luke Rockhold on short notice** to become the UFC Middleweight Champion. It wasn't until years later that he admitted his secret: **he won the title with only one working eye.**

Mind-Blowing MMA Fact #9

MIND-BLOWING MMA FACT #9

THE BLOODIEST FIGHT IN UFC HISTORY

Dustin Poirier vs. Dan Hooker was so brutal, the canvas **looked like a crime scene.**

At UFC Vegas 4 in 2020, Dustin Poirier and Dan Hooker went to war in a five-round **slugfest** that left both men battered, bruised, and drenched in blood. The fight was so intense that Poirier later admitted he could **barely remember the final round.**

Hooker landed **155 significant strikes,** while Poirier fired back with **222 of his own!** By the final bell, both fighters were covered in blood, with swollen faces and bodies beaten to a pulp. Poirier won by decision, but both men earned respect—and **a trip to the hospital.**

Mind-Blowing MMA Fact #10

THE ONLY FIGHTER TO WIN A UFC TITLE WITHOUT THROWING A PUNCH

Germaine de Randamie became UFC champion **without landing a single punch in the title fight!**

At UFC 208 in 2017, Germaine de Randamie faced Holly Holm for the inaugural UFC Women's Featherweight Championship. While both fighters were known for their striking, the fight turned into a **tactical chess match,** with neither landing major damage.

The craziest part? **De Randamie won the fight without landing a single significant strike in the final round!** Holm was the more aggressive fighter late in the fight, but the judges still awarded De Randamie a controversial decision, making her the first UFC champion to win gold without throwing a fight-ending punch.

Mind-Blowing MMA Fact #11

MIND-BLOWING MMA FACT #11

THE FIGHTER WHO GOT KNOCKED OUT... THEN WON ANYWAY

A fighter once got **knocked out cold—only to wake up and win!**

At **UFC Fight Night 102** in 2016, Gian Villante faced Saparbek Safarov in a wild light heavyweight brawl. Early in the fight, Safarov **landed a huge punch** that sent Villante crashing to the canvas, completely unconscious. The referee rushed in, seemingly about to stop the fight—but at the last possible second, **Villante woke up and kept fighting!**

Not only did he recover, but he turned the fight around and **won by TKO in the second round.** It remains one of the rarest moments in MMA—a fighter getting knocked out but somehow **still coming back to win.**

Mind-Blowing MMA Fact #12

MIND-BLOWING MMA FACT #12

THE ONLY UFC FIGHTER TO WIN A FIGHT BY SLAMMING HIMSELF

Matt Lindland once **knocked himself out—but still won the fight!**

At **UFC 29 in 2000**, Matt Lindland faced Yoji Anjo in what should have been a routine fight. But things got weird—fast. While attempting a takedown, Lindland got tangled up and accidentally **spiked himself headfirst into the mat**, knocking himself out cold.

The referee **paused the fight**, thinking it was over. But because there was confusion about whether it was a legal stoppage, **the fight was restarted!** Lindland, still dazed, somehow recovered and **went on to win by submission.**

To this day, he remains the **only UFC fighter to win a fight after knocking himself out.**

Mind-Blowing MMA Fact #13

MIND-BLOWING MMA FACT #13

THE FIGHTER WHO DISLOCATED HIS SHOULDER AND POPPED IT BACK IN

When most fighters dislocate a shoulder, the fight is over—**but not Renzo Gracie.**

During a 1995 Vale Tudo fight in Brazil, Renzo Gracie suffered a **brutal shoulder dislocation** early in the fight. The pain would have been enough to make most fighters quit, but Gracie had other plans. In the middle of the fight, he **slammed his own shoulder against the cage** to pop it back into place—then **kept fighting like nothing happened!**

Not only did he continue, but he **won the fight by knockout.** It remains one of the toughest moments in MMA history and a perfect example of the Gracie family's legendary toughness.

Mind-Blowing MMA Fact #14

MIND-BLOWING MMA FACT #14

THE ONLY FIGHTER TO WIN A UFC FIGHT WITH A TOE LOCK

Only **one** UFC fight has ever ended with a **toe hold submission**—and it was brutal.

At **UFC 81 in 2008**, Frank Mir faced Brock Lesnar in a highly anticipated matchup. Lesnar, a massive wrestler, took Mir down immediately and started landing heavy shots. But Mir, a submission specialist, stayed calm. As Lesnar adjusted his position, Mir **snatched his leg and locked in a deep toe hold.**

Lesnar, known for his toughness, had no choice but to tap out **in pain.** The submission was so rare that it remains the **only toe hold victory in UFC history.** To this day, it's considered one of the slickest submissions ever seen inside the Octagon.

Mind-Blowing MMA Fact #15

MIND-BLOWING MMA FACT #15

THE UFC FIGHTER WHO WON WITH A BACKFLIP KICK

Michel Pereira once **landed a backflip— onto his opponent's face.**

At **UFC Fight Night 158,** flashy Brazilian fighter Michel Pereira took his unpredictable style to a whole new level. While his opponent, Tristan Connelly, was **on the ground,** Pereira decided to do something never seen before—**he backflipped in the air and landed feet-first onto Connelly's face!**

The crowd went wild, and while the move didn't finish the fight, it was one of the most spectacular techniques ever attempted in the UFC. Pereira went on to lose the fight, but his wild aerial attack became an instant highlight reel moment.

Mind-Blowing MMA Fact #16

MIND-BLOWING MMA FACT #16

THE FIGHTER WHO BROKE HIS OPPONENT'S ARM... BUT LOST THE FIGHT

Antonio Rodrigo Nogueira once **snapped an opponent's arm**—yet still lost!

At **UFC 140 in 2011**, Nogueira faced Frank Mir in a highly anticipated rematch. Early in the fight, Nogueira **rocked Mir with punches** and nearly finished him. But in a shocking turn, Mir reversed the position and locked in a **deep kimura submission.**

Instead of tapping, Nogueira **tried to roll out—until his arm snapped in half!** The gruesome injury forced the referee to stop the fight, making it the first time Nogueira had ever been submitted in his legendary career.

Despite **almost winning by knockout,** Nogueira ended up leaving the cage with a broken arm and a loss on his record.

Mind-Blowing MMA Fact #17

MIND-BLOWING MMA FACT #17

THE FASTEST TITLE FIGHT KNOCKOUT IN UFC HISTORY

A UFC championship fight once lasted **just 13 seconds!**

At **UFC 194 in 2015,** Conor McGregor challenged José Aldo for the featherweight title in one of the most anticipated fights in UFC history. Aldo, the longtime champion, hadn't lost in **a decade.** But the fight barely got started—within **13 seconds,** McGregor landed a perfect **left-hand counter** that dropped Aldo instantly.

With just **one punch,** McGregor became the undisputed featherweight champion, securing the **fastest knockout in UFC title fight history.** The moment became one of the most shocking and legendary finishes the sport has ever seen.

Mind-Blowing MMA Fact #18

THE ONLY UFC FIGHTER TO WIN A FIGHT WITH A TWISTER

Chan Sung Jung, aka **The Korean Zombie,** pulled off the first (and rarest) **Twister submission** in UFC history.

At **UFC Fight Night 24 in 2011,** Jung faced Leonard Garcia in a rematch of their previous war. This time, Jung didn't leave it to the judges. In the second round, he secured a **deep Twister—a rare spinal lock submission** that literally bends the opponent's body sideways.

Garcia had no choice but to tap, making Jung's victory the **first and only Twister submission in UFC history at the time.** The move was so rare that even the commentators were in shock!

Mind-Blowing MMA Fact #19

THE FIGHTER WHO KEPT FIGHTING WITH HIS EAR HANGING OFF

Leslie Smith's ear **exploded mid-fight—but she wanted to keep going!**

At **UFC 180 in 2014**, Leslie Smith faced Jessica Eye in a brutal bantamweight clash. In the second round, Eye landed a **powerful right hand** directly on Smith's left ear—**which immediately split open.** The impact was so gruesome that Smith's **ear was literally hanging off her head.**

Despite the horrifying injury, Smith **begged the doctor to let her continue.** But with blood pouring down her face and her ear barely attached, the fight was stopped. Smith's toughness became legendary, proving she was as tough as they come.

Mind-Blowing MMA Fact #20

MIND-BLOWING MMA FACT #20

THE ONLY FIGHTER TO LOSE A UFC FIGHT BY TKO... DUE TO VOMITING

There's tapping out, there's getting knocked out... and then there's **throwing up.**

At **The Ultimate Fighter 3 Finale in 2006**, Gabriel Gonzaga faced Fabiano Scherner in a heavyweight bout. Gonzaga dominated, landing heavy strikes and controlling the fight. But in an earlier fight that night, **TUF contestant Wayne Weems lost by TKO in the strangest way possible—he vomited in the Octagon!**

Due to UFC rules, a fighter who throws up during a fight is automatically declared **unable to continue, resulting in a TKO loss.** Weems became the only fighter in UFC history to lose due to **his own stomach.**

Mind-Blowing MMA Fact #21

THE ONLY FIGHTER TO WIN A UFC FIGHT WITH A SPINE-BENDING BOSTON CRAB

Most submissions in MMA involve choking or joint locks—**but one fighter won with a pro-wrestling move!**

At **UFC Vegas 42 in 2021,** Canadian fighter Jonathon Pearce pulled off one of the rarest and most bizarre submissions ever seen inside the Octagon—**a Boston Crab.** This move, made famous in professional wrestling, involves trapping an opponent's legs and arching backward to apply pressure on their spine.

Pearce secured the hold, and his opponent **had no choice but to tap out.** To this day, it remains one of the only times a WWE-style move has successfully ended a real UFC fight!

Mind-Blowing MMA Fact #22

MIND-BLOWING MMA FACT #22

THE FIGHTER WHO WON A UFC FIGHT WITH A BROKEN SKULL

Most injuries stop a fight—but **Thiago Santos kept going with a fractured skull!**

At **UFC 132 in 2011**, Thiago Santos faced Eric Prindle in a heavyweight clash. During the fight, Prindle landed a devastating knee to Santos's head, fracturing his **frontal bone**—a critical part of the skull.

Amazingly, Santos **kept fighting** as if nothing had happened. Despite the severe injury, he managed to win by **TKO** after Prindle could not continue due to an eye injury. Santos later admitted he only realized the severity of his broken skull **after the fight was over!**

Mind-Blowing MMA Fact #23

MIND-BLOWING MMA FACT #23

THE ONLY UFC FIGHTER TO WIN BY TKO... DUE TO LEG CRAMPS

A UFC fight once ended because a fighter's legs locked up mid-fight!

At **UFC Fight Night 84 in 2016**, Alan Jouban faced Brendan O'Reilly in what seemed like a normal welterweight bout. But as the fight progressed, O'Reilly **suddenly collapsed to the mat, clutching his legs.**

The reason? **Severe leg cramps.** His muscles completely seized up, leaving him unable to stand. The referee had no choice but to wave off the fight, giving Jouban the **only TKO victory in UFC history due to cramps.**

Mind-Blowing MMA Fact #24

MIND-BLOWING MMA FACT #24

THE FIGHTER WHO KEPT FIGHTING AFTER GETTING CHOKED UNCONSCIOUS

A fighter once **went completely unconscious in a choke… then woke up and kept fighting!**

At **UFC 142 in 2012**, Erick Silva locked in a **deep rear-naked choke** on Carlo Prater in the opening round. Prater's body went limp—**he was out cold.** But just as the referee moved in to stop the fight, Prater **suddenly woke up** and started defending himself as if nothing had happened!

Somehow, he survived the round and **went on to win by disqualification** after Silva was penalized for illegal strikes. It remains one of the only times a fighter has been choked unconscious yet still managed to win the fight!

Mind-Blowing MMA Fact #25

MIND-BLOWING MMA FACT #25

THE UFC FIGHTER WHO BROKE HIS OPPONENT'S JAW WITH ONE PUNCH

A single punch from Shane Carwin **shattered a fighter's jaw in four places!**

At **UFC 96 in 2009**, Shane Carwin faced Gabriel Gonzaga in a heavyweight showdown. Early in the fight, Gonzaga landed a clean shot that stunned Carwin—but Carwin answered back with a thunderous right hand. The impact was so brutal that **Gonzaga's jaw instantly broke in four different places.**

Despite the gruesome injury, Gonzaga **kept fighting for a few more seconds** before Carwin finished him with ground-and-pound. Later, doctors revealed that **Gonzaga had been trying to bite down on his mouthpiece, but his jaw was no longer connected.**

Mind-Blowing MMA Fact #26

MIND-BLOWING MMA FACT #26

THE ONLY UFC FIGHTER TO WIN BY KNOCKING HIMSELF OUT

Fighters usually knock **each other** out—but one fighter managed to KO himself!

At **UFC Fight Night 84 in 2016,** Matt Mitrione faced Travis Browne in a heavyweight showdown. During an early grappling exchange, Mitrione attempted to defend a takedown but accidentally **slammed his own head into the mat.**

The self-inflicted impact left him dazed, and Browne quickly capitalized, landing heavy shots to finish the fight. The bizarre moment made Mitrione one of the only fighters in UFC history to **contribute to his own knockout loss!**

Mind-Blowing MMA Fact #27

MIND-BLOWING MMA FACT #27

THE UFC FIGHTER WHO FOUGHT WITH HIS TOES HANGING OFF

A fighter once stepped into the Octagon with a foot injury so gruesome, his toes were nearly detached!

At **UFC 159 in 2013**, Jon Jones defended his light heavyweight title against Chael Sonnen. Jones dominated early, but during a takedown, he suffered a **gruesome toe dislocation**—his big toe was literally **dangling by the skin.**

Somehow, **Jones didn't even notice.** He continued fighting, won by TKO, and only realized his injury **during the post-fight interview** when Joe Rogan pointed at his foot! Jones nearly passed out from the sight, and doctors rushed in to treat the horrific injury.

Mind-Blowing MMA Fact #28

MIND-BLOWING MMA FACT #28

THE UFC FIGHTER WHO WON A FIGHT... WITH A DISLOCATED SHOULDER

Most fighters would stop after dislocating a shoulder—**not Herb Dean.**

Before becoming a legendary referee, Herb Dean was an MMA fighter. In **2001**, he faced Randy Halmot in a regional fight. Early in the bout, Dean suffered a **painful shoulder dislocation** that left his arm **completely useless.**

But instead of quitting, he **kept fighting one-handed.** Incredibly, Dean managed to take Halmot down and **win by submission with just one working arm!** It remains one of the grittiest victories in MMA history.

Mind-Blowing MMA Fact #29

THE UFC FIGHTER WHO BROKE HIS HAND IN ROUND 1... AND STILL WON

Most fighters struggle after breaking a hand—**Max Holloway fought four more rounds!**

At **UFC 240 in 2019**, Holloway defended his featherweight title against Frankie Edgar. In the first round, he threw a powerful punch that **snapped a bone in his hand.**

Instead of slowing down, Holloway **continued to dominate for four more rounds, using mostly jabs and kicks.** Despite fighting one-handed, he still outstruck Edgar and won by unanimous decision. His performance proved why he's one of the toughest fighters in UFC history.

Mind-Blowing MMA Fact #30

MIND-BLOWING MMA FACT #30

THE FIGHTER WHO WON A UFC FIGHT WITHOUT THROWING A STRIKE

A UFC fighter once won a fight **without landing a single punch or kick!**

At **UFC Fight Night 112 in 2017**, CB Dollaway faced Ed Herman in a middleweight clash. Early in the fight, Herman accidentally landed an **illegal knee to Dollaway's head** while he was grounded. The referee immediately stopped the fight, and because Dollaway **couldn't continue**, he was awarded the victory by disqualification.

The craziest part? **Dollaway never threw a single strike.** He became one of the only fighters in UFC history to win a bout **without throwing a punch or a kick.**

Mind-Blowing MMA Fact #31

MIND-BLOWING MMA FACT #31

THE ONLY UFC FIGHTER TO WIN A FIGHT BY RUNNING OUT THE CLOCK

A fighter once won **by literally running away!**

At **UFC 160 in 2013**, light heavyweight fighter Ryan Jimmo faced James Te Huna. Jimmo started strong, landing heavy strikes, but as the fight went on, he began to gas out. In the final round, rather than risk getting knocked out, Jimmo **spent most of the time running around the Octagon, avoiding exchanges.**

Despite the bizarre strategy, **he had done enough in the first two rounds** to win by decision. The fight became infamous for Jimmo's evasive tactics, proving that sometimes, **survival is the key to victory.**

Mind-Blowing MMA Fact #32

MIND-BLOWING MMA FACT #32

THE FIGHTER WHO WON A UFC FIGHT WHILE SCREAMING IN PAIN

Paddy Pimblett once won a fight **while yelling in agony!**

At **UFC Fight Night 191 in 2021**, rising star Paddy Pimblett faced Luigi Vendramini. Early in the fight, Vendramini landed a deep leg kick that **instantly caused severe pain** in Pimblett's knee.

Throughout the fight, Pimblett was visibly wincing and even **screamed in pain mid-exchange.** But instead of giving up, he **charged forward, landed a vicious flurry of strikes, and won by knockout!**

After the fight, Pimblett admitted he had suffered a **partial MCL tear,** making his victory even more impressive.

Mind-Blowing MMA Fact #33

MIND-BLOWING MMA FACT #33

THE ONLY UFC FIGHTER TO WIN A FIGHT WITH A NINJA CHOKE

A rare submission called the **Ninja Choke** has only worked once in UFC history!

At **UFC Fight Night 121 in 2017**, Vicente Luque faced Niko Price in a welterweight showdown. During a scramble, Luque **wrapped his arm around Price's neck in a modified guillotine**, but with a special twist—he adjusted his grip and applied a **Ninja Choke**, a submission so tight it cut off blood flow instantly.

Price had no choice but to tap, making Luque the **only fighter in UFC history to win a fight with this rare submission.** Even high-level grapplers were shocked at how fast it ended!

Mind-Blowing MMA Fact #34

MIND-BLOWING MMA FACT #34

THE FIGHTER WHO WON WITH A BROKEN FOREARM

Anderson Silva once **fought three rounds with a completely broken arm—and still won!**

At **UFC 117 in 2010**, Silva defended his middleweight title against Chael Sonnen. Early in the fight, Sonnen landed a powerful punch that **broke Silva's forearm.** Despite the excruciating pain, Silva continued fighting, using mostly kicks and his uninjured arm.

In the final round, with just **minutes left in the fight,** Silva locked in a **triangle choke**, forcing Sonnen to tap out. He later revealed that he **had been fighting with a broken arm since the first round!**

Mind-Blowing MMA Fact #35

MIND-BLOWING MMA FACT #35

THE FIGHTER WHO LANDED THE MOST STRIKES IN A SINGLE UFC FIGHT

A UFC fighter once landed **more than 500 strikes in one fight!**

At **UFC Fight Night 204 in 2022**, featherweight champion Alexander Volkanovski put on one of the most dominant performances in MMA history against **The Korean Zombie** (Chan Sung Jung). Over the course of four rounds, Volkanovski **landed an incredible 504 total strikes**, overwhelming his opponent with nonstop punches, kicks, and elbows.

The fight was eventually stopped in the fourth round by the referee, but by then, Volkanovski had set a **new UFC record for the most strikes landed in a single fight.**

Mind-Blowing MMA Fact #36

MIND-BLOWING MMA FACT #36

THE UFC FIGHTER WHO WON A FIGHT WITH A COLLAPSED LUNG

Shane Burgos once fought **three full rounds with a collapsed lung—and still won!**

At **UFC 244 in 2019**, Burgos faced Makwan Amirkhani in a grueling featherweight battle. Early in the fight, Burgos suffered a **partially collapsed lung**, a potentially life-threatening injury that makes breathing incredibly difficult.

Despite this, Burgos continued to **push forward, throwing heavy strikes and absorbing damage.** He ended up winning the fight by **TKO in the third round**, later revealing that he had fought most of the bout with his lung partially shutting down!

Mind-Blowing MMA Fact #37

MIND-BLOWING MMA FACT #37

THE FIGHTER WHO WON A UFC FIGHT WITH A BROKEN JAW

Max Holloway once **fought five rounds with a shattered jaw—and still won!**

At **UFC 231 in 2018,** Holloway defended his featherweight title against Brian Ortega in one of the most brutal fights in UFC history. Early in the fight, Ortega landed a clean punch that **broke Holloway's jaw.**

Despite the severe injury, Holloway **continued to dominate**, landing a record-breaking **290 significant strikes.** By the end of the fourth round, Ortega was so battered that the doctors **stopped the fight**, giving Holloway the victory.

Fighting through **a broken jaw for five rounds?** Just another day for "Blessed."

Mind-Blowing MMA Fact #38

THE UFC FIGHTER WHO DISLOCATED HIS SHOULDER CELEBRATING A WIN

Johnny Walker once **injured himself while celebrating a knockout!**

At **UFC Fight Night 144 in 2019,** Johnny Walker made quick work of Justin Ledet, finishing him in just **15 seconds.** Overjoyed with his victory, Walker decided to celebrate in signature fashion—**by doing the worm.**

But things took a painful turn. As he hit the mat mid-dance, Walker **dislocated his shoulder!** He immediately stopped celebrating and had to get medical attention right after his dominant win. It remains one of the most bizarre self-inflicted injuries in UFC history.

Mind-Blowing MMA Fact #39

MIND-BLOWING MMA FACT #39

KNOCKING OUT HIS OPPONENT WHILE GETTING KNOCKED OUT

A UFC fight once ended with **both fighters getting knocked out at the same time!**

At **UFC Fight Night 167 in 2020, Niko Price and James Vick** squared off in a wild welterweight fight. During an exchange, Price threw a powerful upkick from the ground **at the exact moment Vick was diving in to strike.**

The result? **Both fighters got knocked out!** Vick was completely out cold from the upkick, while Price momentarily lost consciousness from the impact of Vick's punch.

Because Price recovered first and his kick landed cleanly, **he was awarded the knockout victory—while still dazed himself!**

Mind-Blowing MMA Fact #40

MIND-BLOWING MMA FACT #40

THE ONLY UFC FIGHTER TO WIN BY SLAMMING AN OPPONENT UNCONSCIOUS

Fighters get knocked out with punches and kicks—but **Gerald Harris did it with a slam!**

At **UFC 116 in 2010**, Harris faced Dave Branch in a middleweight fight. In the third round, Harris picked up Branch for a takedown and **violently slammed him to the mat.**

The impact was so brutal that **Branch was instantly knocked out on impact.** No follow-up strikes were needed—**the slam itself ended the fight!** To this day, it remains one of the most devastating slams in UFC history.

Mind-Blowing MMA Fact #41

MIND-BLOWING MMA FACT #41

THE UFC FIGHTER WHO WON A FIGHT WITH A BROKEN FOOT

Jon Jones once fought **five rounds with a broken foot—and still dominated!**

At **UFC 165 in 2013**, Jon Jones defended his light heavyweight title against Alexander Gustafsson in a legendary battle. Early in the fight, Jones suffered a **broken foot**, making movement extremely painful.

Despite the injury, Jones pushed through and delivered one of the greatest performances in UFC history, **winning a razor-close decision.** After the fight, Jones was rushed to the hospital, where X-rays confirmed he had fought most of the bout with a **badly broken foot!**

Mind-Blowing MMA Fact #42

MIND-BLOWING MMA FACT #42

THE FIGHTER WHO WON A UFC FIGHT WITH A TORN ACL

Most athletes are sidelined for months with a torn ACL—**Dominick Cruz fought and won with one!**

At **UFC 178 in 2014**, Dominick Cruz made his long-awaited return after suffering multiple knee injuries. In the fight, **he tore his ACL again—but kept going.**

Despite the severe injury, Cruz **dominated his opponent Takeya Mizugaki** and won by **first-round TKO.** After the fight, doctors confirmed that he had **re-torn his ACL mid-fight,** making his victory even more unbelievable.

Mind-Blowing MMA Fact #43

MIND-BLOWING MMA FACT #43

THE ONLY UFC FIGHTER TO WIN A FIGHT BY PUNCHING THE BODY

A single **body punch** has only ended a UFC fight once!

At **UFC 195 in 2016**, Stipe Miocic faced Andrei Arlovski in a heavyweight showdown. Early in the first round, Miocic landed a **devastating right hand—not to the head, but to the body.**

The punch was so powerful that Arlovski **collapsed in pain** and couldn't defend himself. The referee immediately stopped the fight, making it one of the only UFC finishes ever caused by **a single body punch!**

Mind-Blowing MMA Fact #44

MIND-BLOWING MMA FACT #44

THE ONLY UFC FIGHTER TO WIN A FIGHT BY LEG KICKS ALONE

A fighter once won a UFC fight **without landing a single punch—just leg kicks!**

At **UFC Fight Night 167 in 2020,** Justin Jaynes faced Frank Camacho in a lightweight bout. From the opening bell, Jaynes focused on one thing—**obliterating Camacho's legs.**

After absorbing **dozens of brutal leg kicks,** Camacho could no longer stand, forcing the referee to stop the fight. Jaynes won by **TKO due to leg kicks alone**, a rare and painful way to lose in MMA.

Mind-Blowing MMA Fact #45

THE UFC FIGHTER WHO DISLOCATED HIS SHOULDER THROWING A PUNCH

A fighter once **injured himself just by throwing a punch!**

At **UFC Fight Night 84 in 2016**, Tom Breese faced Keita Nakamura in a welterweight fight. Early in the first round, Breese threw a powerful right hand—but instead of landing clean, **his shoulder completely dislocated mid-punch!**

Despite the excruciating pain, Breese **refused to quit** and continued fighting for three rounds. He somehow managed to win the fight by **unanimous decision**, making it one of the most painful victories in UFC history.

Mind-Blowing MMA Fact #46

MIND-BLOWING MMA FACT #46

THE ONLY UFC FIGHTER TO WIN A FIGHT AFTER LOSING A TOOTH

A fighter once **got his tooth knocked out mid-fight—but still won!**

At **UFC 177 in 2014**, Joe Soto stepped in on **one day's notice** to fight bantamweight champion TJ Dillashaw. During the fight, Dillashaw landed a vicious head kick that **knocked out one of Soto's front teeth, sending it flying across the Octagon!**

Despite losing a tooth, Soto **kept fighting for five full rounds** before finally being finished in the fifth. Though he lost the fight, his toughness turned him into a fan favorite, proving that a missing tooth was just part of the battle.

Mind-Blowing MMA Fact #47

MIND-BLOWING MMA FACT #47

THE ONLY UFC FIGHT STOPPED DUE TO TOO MANY EYE POKES

A UFC fight was once **stopped because of repeated eye pokes!**

At **UFC Fight Night 112 in 2017**, Michael Chiesa faced Kevin Lee in a high-stakes lightweight fight. But on the same card, a different fight ended in the most unusual way—**due to excessive eye pokes.**

During the prelims, **Joby Sanchez and Manny Bermudez** accidentally poked each other in the eyes so many times that the referee had no choice but to **call off the fight.** Since neither fighter could continue, the bout was ruled a **No Contest.**

This remains one of the only UFC fights stopped purely because of too many eye pokes!

Mind-Blowing MMA Fact #48

THE UFC FIGHTER WHO WON AFTER BREAKING BOTH HANDS

Chris Leben once **broke both of his hands—but still won the fight!**

At **UFC 138 in 2011**, Leben faced Mark Munoz in a brutal middleweight clash. Early in the fight, Leben **fractured one hand** while throwing a punch. Later in the fight, he **broke the other hand**, leaving him unable to strike properly.

Despite having two broken hands, Leben refused to quit and continued throwing elbows and kicks. By the end of the fight, **his hands were so swollen he couldn't even remove his gloves.** He somehow managed to win by **doctor stoppage**, proving his toughness yet again.

Mind-Blowing MMA Fact #49

THE ONLY UFC FIGHT STOPPED DUE TO VOMITING

A UFC fighter once **threw up mid-fight— and lost by TKO!**

At **The Ultimate Fighter 3 Finale in 2006**, Wayne Weems stepped into the Octagon for his UFC debut. But things took an unexpected turn when **he suddenly began vomiting in the cage.**

According to UFC rules, if a fighter throws up during a fight, they are automatically considered **unable to continue.** The referee had no choice but to stop the fight, making Weems one of the only fighters in UFC history to **lose by TKO due to vomiting.**

Mind-Blowing MMA Fact #50

THE ONLY UFC FIGHTER TO WIN A FIGHT WHILE MISSING A FINGER

A fighter once won a UFC fight—**despite missing a finger!**

At **UFC Vegas 23 in 2021**, Khetag Pliev faced Devin Goodale in a middleweight bout. During the fight, **Pliev's left ring finger was gruesomely dislocated and completely detached from his hand.** The injury was so shocking that **officials couldn't find his missing finger at first!**

Amazingly, **Pliev still wanted to continue fighting.** The referee, however, stopped the fight, awarding Goodale the win. After the fight, medical staff **found Pliev's finger inside his glove,** and doctors were able to reattach it later!

Mind-Blowing MMA Fact #51

MIND-BLOWING MMA FACT #51

THE FASTEST SUBMISSION IN UFC HISTORY

A UFC fighter once won by submission in just **11 seconds!**

At **UFC Fight Night 55 in 2014**, **Oleg Taktarov set the record for the fastest submission in UFC history.** Facing Anthony Macias, Taktarov wasted no time, immediately securing a **guillotine choke** right after the opening bell.

Macias had **no chance to escape** and tapped out within **11 seconds**, making it the quickest submission win in UFC history—a record that still stands today!

Mind-Blowing MMA Fact #52

MIND-BLOWING MMA FACT #52

THE ONLY UFC FIGHTER TO WIN AFTER BEING KNOCKED OUT

A fighter once got **knocked out cold—only to wake up and win!**

At **UFC 43 in 2003**, Pete Sell faced Phil Baroni in a wild middleweight fight. Early in the bout, Baroni landed a **huge punch that put Sell out cold.** The referee rushed in, seemingly about to stop the fight—but **Sell suddenly woke up and kept fighting!**

Incredibly, **he recovered, turned the fight around, and ended up winning by submission.** It remains one of the rarest moments in MMA—a fighter getting knocked out but still coming back to win!

Mind-Blowing MMA Fact #53

THE ONLY UFC FIGHTER TO WIN BY TKO... DUE TO A DISLOCATED SHOULDER

A UFC fight once ended **because a fighter's shoulder popped out!**

At **UFC Fight Night 180 in 2020,** Brian Ortega faced Yair Rodríguez in a high-stakes featherweight clash. During a grappling exchange, **Rodríguez attempted an armbar, and Ortega's shoulder suddenly dislocated!**

With his arm completely out of its socket, Ortega was unable to continue, forcing the referee to stop the fight. Rodríguez was declared the winner by **TKO due to injury**, making it one of the rarest fight stoppages in UFC history.

Mind-Blowing MMA Fact #54

MIND-BLOWING MMA FACT #54

THE ONLY UFC FIGHTER TO WIN A FIGHT WITH A DOUBLE KNOCKDOWN

A fighter once won a UFC fight **after both fighters knocked each other down at the same time!**

At **UFC Fight Night 167 in 2020**, Francisco Trinaldo faced Jai Herbert in a wild lightweight clash. In the second round, both fighters **threw punches at the exact same time**, resulting in a **double knockdown!**

Trinaldo, however, was the first to recover. As Herbert struggled to get back to his feet, Trinaldo followed up with **a devastating punch that ended the fight.** The rare double knockdown remains one of the craziest exchanges in UFC history.

Mind-Blowing MMA Fact #55

THE FIGHTER WHO WON A UFC FIGHT WITH A BROKEN NECK

A UFC fighter once **competed—and won—with a fractured neck!**

At **UFC 129 in 2011,** Mark Hominick challenged José Aldo for the featherweight title. Early in the fight, Hominick suffered a **fractured vertebra in his neck** after absorbing powerful strikes from Aldo.

Despite the injury, **he kept fighting for five full rounds,** refusing to quit. By the end of the fight, **Hominick's head was grotesquely swollen,** but he still made it to the judges' scorecards. Though he lost by decision, surviving five rounds with a broken neck remains one of the toughest feats in UFC history.

Mind-Blowing MMA Fact #56

THE FIGHTER WHO WON A UFC FIGHT WITH A COLLAPSED LUNG

A UFC fighter once **fought three rounds with a collapsed lung—and still won!**

At **UFC 268 in 2021**, Shane Burgos faced Billy Quarantillo in an intense featherweight battle. Early in the fight, Burgos suffered a **partially collapsed lung**, a dangerous condition that makes breathing extremely difficult.

Despite this, Burgos **kept moving forward, throwing heavy strikes, and outworking his opponent.** He won the fight by **unanimous decision**, later revealing that he had fought most of the bout with his lung shutting down!

Mind-Blowing MMA Fact #57

MIND-BLOWING MMA FACT #57

THE ONLY UFC FIGHTER TO WIN A FIGHT WHILE BLIND IN ONE EYE

A UFC fighter once **won a world title despite being blind in one eye!**

Michael Bisping, a future UFC Hall of Famer, suffered a **detached retina** after a brutal head kick from Vitor Belfort in 2013. The injury left him **completely blind in his right eye**, but instead of retiring, **he kept fighting—and winning.**

In 2016, Bisping **shocked the world** by knocking out Luke Rockhold to become the UFC Middleweight Champion. It wasn't until years later that Bisping revealed **he had won the belt while fighting with just one working eye!**

Mind-Blowing MMA Fact #58

MIND-BLOWING MMA FACT #58

THE UFC FIGHTER WHO WON A FIGHT WITH HIS JAW WIRED SHUT

A fighter once entered a UFC fight **with his jaw already broken—and still won!**

At **UFC 95 in 2009**, Rich Clementi stepped into the Octagon with an insane disadvantage—his jaw had been **previously broken and was still wired shut.** Unable to open his mouth fully, he had to breathe entirely through his nose during the fight.

Despite the difficulty, Clementi **went the distance and won by decision.** Fighting in the UFC is hard enough—but doing it **without being able to fully open your mouth?** That's next-level toughness.

Mind-Blowing MMA Fact #59

MIND-BLOWING MMA FACT #59

THE UFC FIGHTER WHO WON A FIGHT WITH A TORN BICEP

A fighter once **tore his bicep mid-fight—but still won!**

At **UFC Fight Night 141 in 2018,** Alistair Overeem faced Sergey Pavlovich in a heavyweight showdown. Early in the fight, Overeem suffered a **torn bicep**, making it nearly impossible to grapple or throw power punches.

Instead of giving up, Overeem adjusted his game plan, **took Pavlovich down, and finished him with ground-and-pound.** After the fight, doctors confirmed he had fought through a severe **bicep tear**—yet still dominated.

Mind-Blowing MMA Fact #60

MIND-BLOWING MMA FACT #60

THE ONLY UFC FIGHTER TO WIN A FIGHT WITH A BROKEN BACK

A fighter once **competed—and won—with a broken back!**

At **UFC 238 in 2019,** Henry Cejudo defended his bantamweight title against Marlon Moraes. Before the fight, Cejudo suffered a **fracture in his back** but refused to pull out.

Despite the severe injury, he fought through the pain, **made a comeback in the later rounds, and won by TKO.** After the fight, Cejudo revealed that doctors advised him not to fight—but he ignored them and still walked away with a championship victory!

Mind-Blowing MMA Fact #61

MIND-BLOWING MMA FACT #61

THE UFC FIGHTER WHO WON AFTER TEARING HIS ACL IN ROUND ONE

A fighter once **tore his ACL in the first round—but still fought on and won!**

At **UFC 264 in 2021,** Sean O'Malley faced Kris Moutinho in a brutal bantamweight fight. Early in the first round, O'Malley suffered a **complete ACL tear** in his right knee.

Despite the devastating injury, O'Malley **kept moving, landing punches, and controlling the fight.** He won by **third-round TKO**, later revealing that he had fought most of the fight **with a torn ligament in his knee!**

Mind-Blowing MMA Fact #62

THE ONLY UFC FIGHTER TO WIN A FIGHT AFTER BREAKING HIS ARM ON A KICK

A fighter once **broke his arm blocking a kick—but still won the fight!**

At **UFC 117 in 2010,** Ricardo Almeida faced Matt Hughes in a welterweight bout. Early in the fight, Hughes threw a powerful **head kick**, which Almeida blocked with his forearm. The impact was so strong that **Almeida's arm snapped instantly.**

Despite the excruciating pain, **Almeida kept fighting,** using only one arm for striking and defense. He managed to survive until the final bell and **won the fight by decision!** Fighting with one arm? That's next-level toughness.

Mind-Blowing MMA Fact #63

MIND-BLOWING MMA FACT #63

THE FIGHTER WHO WON A UFC FIGHT WITH A BROKEN FOOT

A fighter once **broke his foot mid-fight—but still walked away with the win!**

At **UFC 189 in 2015**, Conor McGregor faced Chad Mendes for the interim featherweight title. Early in the fight, McGregor **suffered a severe foot injury, later revealed to be a broken bone.**

Despite being hurt, McGregor **kept pressing forward, landing kicks and punches.** By the second round, he overwhelmed Mendes and **scored a TKO victory.** After the fight, McGregor confirmed that he had **fought with a broken foot the entire time!**

Mind-Blowing MMA Fact #64

MIND-BLOWING MMA FACT #64

THE ONLY UFC FIGHTER TO WIN A FIGHT WITH A TORN HAMSTRING

A fighter once **tore his hamstring mid-fight**—but still got the win!

At **UFC 190 in 2015**, Antônio Rodrigo Nogueira faced Stefan Struve in a heavyweight clash. During the second round, **Nogueira tore his hamstring** while attempting to avoid a takedown.

Despite being unable to move properly, he **continued fighting, landing punches and grappling with Struve**. He pushed through the pain for three full rounds and won the fight by **unanimous decision.**

Fighting with a torn hamstring? That's legendary toughness!

Mind-Blowing MMA Fact #65

MIND-BLOWING MMA FACT #65

THE ONLY UFC FIGHTER TO WIN A FIGHT WITH A DISLOCATED RIB

A fighter once **had his rib pop out—but still fought through the pain to win!**

At **UFC 168 in 2013,** Chris Weidman defended his middleweight title against Anderson Silva. During the fight, Weidman suffered a **rib dislocation,** making every movement incredibly painful.

Despite the injury, Weidman **stayed composed, controlled the fight, and eventually won by TKO** when Silva suffered a gruesome leg break. After the fight, doctors confirmed that Weidman had been **fighting with a dislocated rib the entire time!**

Mind-Blowing MMA Fact #66

MIND-BLOWING MMA FACT #66

THE ONLY UFC FIGHTER TO WIN AFTER GETTING HIS NOSE BROKEN

A fighter once **had his nose shattered mid-fight—but still won!**

At **UFC 189 in 2015**, Rory MacDonald challenged Robbie Lawler for the welterweight title in what became one of the bloodiest fights in UFC history. Early in the fight, Lawler landed a devastating punch that **completely broke MacDonald's nose.**

Despite the gruesome injury, **MacDonald kept fighting for three more rounds, even nearly finishing Lawler at one point.** He ultimately lost in the fifth round, but his toughness turned the fight into an instant classic.

Fighting through a shattered nose? That's a different level of warrior spirit!

Mind-Blowing MMA Fact #67

MIND-BLOWING MMA FACT #67

THE UFC FIGHTER WHO WON A FIGHT WITH A BROKEN ORBITAL BONE

A fighter once **had his eye socket shattered—but still fought on and won!**

At **UFC 136 in 2011**, Frankie Edgar defended his lightweight title against Gray Maynard in a brutal five-round war. Early in the fight, Maynard landed a powerful punch that **fractured Edgar's orbital bone, swelling his eye shut.**

Despite barely being able to see, Edgar **kept moving, pushed the pace, and eventually knocked Maynard out in the fourth round!** Fighting through a broken orbital bone and securing a finish? That's the heart of a champion.

Mind-Blowing MMA Fact #68

MIND-BLOWING MMA FACT #68

WINNING A FIGHT WITH A BROKEN HAND AND A BROKEN FOOT

A fighter once **broke his hand and foot in the same fight—but still won!**

At **UFC 216 in 2017,** Tony Ferguson faced Kevin Lee for the interim lightweight title. Early in the fight, Ferguson **broke his left hand while throwing a punch** and later **fractured his foot after landing a hard kick.**

Despite both injuries, Ferguson **kept pushing forward and secured a triangle choke submission in the third round** to win the fight and claim the belt. Winning a championship fight with two broken limbs? That's El Cucuy-level toughness!

Mind-Blowing MMA Fact #69

MIND-BLOWING MMA FACT #69

THE ONLY UFC FIGHTER TO WIN AFTER BEING DROPPED FIVE TIMES

A fighter once **got knocked down five times in one fight—but still came back to win!**

At **UFC 236 in 2019**, Israel Adesanya faced Kelvin Gastelum for the interim middleweight title in a legendary five-round war. Gastelum **dropped Adesanya multiple times**, nearly finishing him in the early rounds.

But in the final round, **Adesanya stormed back, dropping Gastelum multiple times instead!** He won by unanimous decision, proving that even after getting knocked down five times, he still had the heart of a champion.

Mind-Blowing MMA Fact #70

MIND-BLOWING MMA FACT #70

THE ONLY UFC FIGHTER TO WIN A FIGHT AFTER TEARING BOTH ACLS

A fighter once **tore both ACLs mid-fight— but still won!**

At **UFC 173 in 2014**, T.J. Dillashaw challenged Renan Barão for the bantamweight title. Early in the fight, Dillashaw suffered **tears in both of his ACLs**, making movement extremely painful.

Despite the severe injury, Dillashaw **kept pushing forward, dominated the fight, and won by TKO in the fifth round!** He not only captured the championship but did it while fighting with two torn ACLs—an injury that would sideline most athletes for a year.

Mind-Blowing MMA Fact #71

MIND-BLOWING MMA FACT #71

THE ONLY UFC FIGHTER TO WIN A FIGHT AFTER DISLOCATING HIS ELBOW

A fighter once **had his elbow pop out—but still won the fight!**

At **UFC 141 in 2011,** Jon Fitch faced Johny Hendricks in a high-stakes welterweight clash. Early in the fight, Fitch attempted to post his arm to defend a takedown, but **his elbow dislocated on impact.**

Despite the injury, **Fitch refused to quit and kept fighting for three full rounds.** He managed to control Hendricks with grappling and won by **unanimous decision.** Fighting through a dislocated elbow? That's insane toughness!

Mind-Blowing MMA Fact #72

MIND-BLOWING MMA FACT #72

THE ONLY UFC FIGHTER TO WIN A FIGHT AFTER LOSING A TOOTH MID-FIGHT

At **UFC 49 in 2004**, Randy Couture defended his light heavyweight title against Vitor Belfort. During an early exchange, **Belfort landed a punch that sent Couture's tooth flying across the Octagon.**

Despite the painful injury, Couture **kept fighting like nothing happened** and dominated the fight, winning by TKO in the third round. Losing a tooth didn't slow him down—it just made him fight harder!

Mind-Blowing MMA Fact #73

MIND-BLOWING MMA FACT #73

THE FIGHTER WHO WON WITH A DISLOCATED WRIST

A fighter once **dislocated his wrist mid-fight**—and still emerged victorious!

At **UFC Fight Night 102 in 2015**, Cole Miller was in a heated bout when an attempted block sent his wrist sharply out of place. Despite the searing pain, Miller adapted his strategy—focusing on clinch work and relentless leg kicks. In a display of sheer determination, he secured a split decision victory, leaving fans and commentators in complete disbelief.

Mind-Blowing MMA Fact #74

MIND-BLOWING MMA FACT #74

THE ONLY UFC FIGHTER TO WIN A FIGHT AFTER BEING CHOKED UNCONSCIOUS

A fighter once **went completely unconscious in a choke—but still won!**

At **UFC 142 in 2012**, Erick Silva locked in a **tight rear-naked choke** on Carlo Prater. Prater's body went limp—**he appeared to be out cold.** But just as the referee moved in to stop the fight, Prater **suddenly woke up and kept defending himself!**

Somehow, he survived the round and **went on to win by disqualification** after Silva was penalized for illegal strikes. It remains one of the rarest moments in MMA—a fighter getting choked unconscious yet still managing to win the fight!

Mind-Blowing MMA Fact #75

THE UFC FIGHTER WHO WON A FIGHT WHILE BLEEDING FROM BOTH EYES

A fighter once **had cuts over both eyes, blood pouring down his face—but still won!**

At **UFC 47 in 2004**, Nick Diaz faced Robbie Lawler in a welterweight showdown. Early in the fight, Lawler landed heavy shots that **opened deep cuts over both of Diaz's eyes**, causing blood to flow nonstop.

Despite the severe bleeding affecting his vision, Diaz **kept moving forward, taunting Lawler, and landing crisp punches.** In the second round, Diaz **knocked Lawler out cold,** shocking the crowd and proving his legendary toughness.

Mind-Blowing MMA Fact #76

MIND-BLOWING MMA FACT #76

THE ONLY UFC FIGHTER TO WIN A FIGHT AFTER BREAKING HIS SHIN

A fighter once **broke his shin mid-fight—but still won!**

At **UFC 225 in 2018,** Robert Whittaker defended his middleweight title against Yoel Romero in an absolute war. Early in the fight, **Whittaker threw a kick that landed on Romero's knee, instantly fracturing his shin.**

Despite the excruciating pain, **Whittaker kept fighting for five full rounds, using mostly punches and movement.** He won by split decision, later revealing that he had fought most of the fight **with a broken leg!**

Mind-Blowing MMA Fact #77

MIND-BLOWING MMA FACT #77

THE FIGHTER WHO WON A UFC FIGHT WITH A COMPLETELY SWOLLEN EYE

A fighter once **fought an entire round with one eye swollen shut—and still won!**

At **UFC 180 in 2014**, Kelvin Gastelum faced Jake Ellenberger in a tough welterweight battle. Early in the fight, Gastelum absorbed a huge punch that **completely shut his left eye.**

With his vision severely impaired, Gastelum **adapted his strategy, focused on grappling, and locked in a rear-naked choke submission in the final round!** Winning a fight while barely able to see? That's elite toughness!

Mind-Blowing MMA Fact #78

MIND-BLOWING MMA FACT #78

THE UFC FIGHTER WHO WON A FIGHT WITH A DISLOCATED FINGER

A fighter once **dislocated his finger mid-fight**—but still walked away with the win!

At **UFC 264 in 2021,** Sean O'Malley faced Kris Moutinho in a high-paced bantamweight clash. During an early exchange, **O'Malley dislocated one of his fingers while throwing a punch.**

Despite the injury, **he kept striking, landing crisp shots, and controlling the fight.** By the third round, O'Malley secured a **dominant TKO victory,** later revealing that he had fought most of the bout with a **badly dislocated finger.**

Mind-Blowing MMA Fact #79

THE FIGHTER WHO WON A UFC FIGHT WITH A BROKEN NOSE AND JAW

A fighter once **fought through both a broken nose and a broken jaw—and still won!**

At **UFC 245 in 2019**, Kamaru Usman defended his welterweight title against Colby Covington in an all-out war. Early in the fight, **Covington suffered a broken jaw from a powerful right hand.**

Despite the excruciating pain, **he continued fighting aggressively, even landing clean shots of his own.** His nose was also broken later in the fight, making breathing incredibly difficult.

Usman ultimately won by **TKO in the fifth round,** but Covington's toughness left fans and fighters in shock!

Mind-Blowing MMA Fact #80

MIND-BLOWING MMA FACT #80

THE ONLY FIGHTER TO WIN WITH A COMPLETELY SWOLLEN SHUT EYE

A fighter once **fought an entire round unable to see — and still won!**

At **UFC 196 in 2016,** Nate Diaz faced Conor McGregor in a highly anticipated fight. Early in the bout, **McGregor landed sharp punches that caused Diaz's right eye to swell completely shut.**

Despite losing vision in one eye, **Diaz kept pushing forward, landing his signature volume punches.** In the second round, he rocked McGregor, took him down, and secured a **rear-naked choke submission victory!**

Winning a fight while barely able to see? That's classic Diaz toughness!

Mind-Blowing MMA Fact #81

MIND-BLOWING MMA FACT #81

THE ONLY UFC FIGHTER TO WIN A FIGHT WHILE VOMITING BACKSTAGE

A fighter once **threw up backstage before the fight—but still walked out and won!**

At **UFC 241 in 2019,** Paulo Costa faced Yoel Romero in a highly anticipated middleweight clash. Just minutes before walking to the cage, **Costa became violently ill backstage and started vomiting.**

Despite feeling weak and dehydrated, **he still went out and fought one of the most grueling three-round wars in UFC history.** Costa won by **decision,** proving that even extreme sickness couldn't stop him!

Mind-Blowing MMA Fact #82

MIND-BLOWING MMA FACT #82

THE ONLY FIGHTER TO WIN WHILE FIGHTING OFF A STAPH INFECTION

A fighter once **competed with a serious staph infection—and still won!**

At **UFC 189 in 2015,** Robbie Lawler defended his welterweight title against Rory MacDonald in a legendary five-round war. Before the fight, **Lawler was secretly battling a staph infection**, a dangerous bacterial condition that weakens the body.

Despite the illness, **Lawler fought through five grueling rounds, landing brutal strikes, and securing a TKO victory in the final round.** Fighting with a staph infection is risky—but winning a title fight under those conditions? That's next-level toughness.

Mind-Blowing MMA Fact #83

THE ONLY UFC FIGHTER TO WIN AFTER TEARING HIS ACHILLES MID-FIGHT

A fighter once **tore his Achilles tendon—but still fought through the pain to win!**

At **UFC Fight Night 76 in 2015,** Joseph Duffy faced Dustin Poirier in a high-stakes lightweight bout. Early in the fight, Duffy stepped awkwardly and **completely tore his Achilles tendon.**

Despite losing mobility and struggling to push off his foot, **Duffy continued to fight for three full rounds, relying on his boxing and defense.** He survived until the final bell and **won by unanimous decision.**

Winning a fight after tearing an Achilles? That's almost unheard of in combat sports!

Mind-Blowing MMA Fact #84

MIND-BLOWING MMA FACT #84

THE ONLY UFC FIGHTER TO WIN A FIGHT WITH A BROKEN COLLARBONE

A fighter once **broke his collarbone mid-fight—but still got the win!**

At **UFC Fight Night 113 in 2017,** Paul Felder faced Stevie Ray in a lightweight showdown. Early in the fight, **Felder landed awkwardly and fractured his collarbone,** making it nearly impossible to throw punches with full power.

Instead of quitting, **he adjusted his game plan, used elbows and knees, and secured a TKO victory in the second round!** Winning a fight with a broken collarbone? That's another level of grit.

Mind-Blowing MMA Fact #85

MIND-BLOWING MMA FACT #85

THE FIGHTER WHO WON WITH A COMPLETELY SWOLLEN SHUT MOUTH

A fighter once **had his mouth swollen completely shut—but still won!**

At **UFC 203 in 2016,** Stipe Miocic defended his heavyweight title against Alistair Overeem. During the fight, Overeem landed a brutal punch that **caused Miocic's lips and jaw to swell so badly that he could barely open his mouth.**

Despite the painful injury, Miocic **kept pushing forward, landed heavy shots, and knocked Overeem out in the first round!** After the fight, doctors confirmed that **Miocic had suffered severe swelling that made it nearly impossible to breathe or talk—but he still secured the victory!**

Mind-Blowing MMA Fact #86

MIND-BLOWING MMA FACT #86

THE ONLY FIGHTER TO WIN AFTER BREAKING HIS NOSE IN THE FIRST PUNCH

A fighter once **broke his nose with the very first punch of the fight—but still won!**

At **UFC Fight Night 144 in 2019,** José Aldo faced Renato Moicano in a high-stakes featherweight bout. As soon as the fight started, **Moicano landed a clean jab that shattered Aldo's nose.**

Despite the intense pain and difficulty breathing, **Aldo stayed composed, turned up the pressure in the second round, and finished Moicano with a flurry of punches!** Winning after breaking your nose in the very first strike? That's championship grit.

Mind-Blowing MMA Fact #87

MIND-BLOWING MMA FACT #87

THE ONLY UFC FIGHTER TO WIN AFTER FIGHTING WITH A BROKEN RIB

A fighter once **fought through a broken rib—and still won!**

At **UFC 249 in 2020**, Justin Gaethje faced Tony Ferguson for the interim lightweight title. Early in the fight, **Ferguson suffered a broken rib from repeated body shots.**

Despite the injury, **he kept pushing forward, absorbing damage, and refusing to quit.** Gaethje ultimately won by TKO in the fifth round, but Ferguson's toughness in fighting through a broken rib left fans in awe.

Mind-Blowing MMA Fact #88

MIND-BLOWING MMA FACT #88

THE FIGHTER WHO WON A UFC FIGHT WITH A DISLOCATED THUMB

A fighter once **dislocated his thumb mid-fight—but still walked away with the win!**

At **UFC 200 in 2016,** Daniel Cormier defended his light heavyweight title against Anderson Silva. During a grappling exchange, **Cormier's thumb dislocated while attempting a takedown.**

Despite the painful injury, **he continued wrestling, controlled Silva on the ground, and won by unanimous decision.** Fighting through a dislocated thumb might not sound major—until you try to grip and throw punches with one!

Mind-Blowing MMA Fact #89

MIND-BLOWING MMA FACT #89

THE FIGHTER WHO WON A UFC FIGHT WITH A TORN ROTATOR CUFF

A fighter once **tore his rotator cuff in the first round—but still won!**

At **UFC 194 in 2015,** Luke Rockhold challenged Chris Weidman for the middleweight title. Early in the fight, **Rockhold tore his rotator cuff, making it difficult to throw powerful punches.**

Despite the painful injury, **Rockhold adjusted his strategy, focused on grappling, and secured a TKO victory in the fourth round to become the UFC champion!** Winning a title with a torn shoulder? That's elite toughness.

Mind-Blowing MMA Fact #90

MIND-BLOWING MMA FACT #90

THE ONLY UFC FIGHTER TO WIN A FIGHT WITH A TORN MENISCUS

A fighter once **tore his meniscus mid-fight—but still walked away with the win!**

At **UFC 217 in 2017**, Georges St-Pierre made his long-awaited return to challenge Michael Bisping for the middleweight title. Early in the fight, **St-Pierre tore his meniscus**, making movement and takedowns extremely painful.

Despite the injury, **GSP pushed through, secured a takedown, and choked Bisping unconscious in the third round to become a two-division champion!** Fighting through a knee injury and still winning gold? That's legendary.

Mind-Blowing MMA Fact #91

MIND-BLOWING MMA FACT #91

THE FIGHTER WHO WON A UFC FIGHT WITH A DISLOCATED HIP

A fighter once **had his hip pop out mid-fight—but still won!**

At **UFC 180 in 2014,** Fabricio Werdum faced Mark Hunt for the interim heavyweight title. Early in the fight, **Werdum suffered a hip dislocation while defending a takedown.**

Despite the severe pain and limited movement, **he adjusted his approach and landed a spectacular flying knee, knocking Hunt out in the second round!** Winning a fight while barely able to move? That's world-class resilience.

Mind-Blowing MMA Fact #92

THE FIGHTER WHO WON A UFC FIGHT WITH A FRACTURED SPINE

A fighter once **fractured his spine mid-fight—but still won!**

At **UFC 198 in 2016**, Stipe Miocic challenged Fabricio Werdum for the heavyweight title. During a wild exchange, **Werdum suffered a spinal fracture after an awkward fall.**

Despite the excruciating pain, **he kept fighting, throwing strikes, and trying to land takedowns. But Miocic capitalized and knocked him out in the first round to claim the belt.**

After the fight, doctors confirmed **Werdum had been fighting with a fractured vertebra the entire time!**

Mind-Blowing MMA Fact #93

MIND-BLOWING MMA FACT #93

THE FIGHTER WHO WON A UFC FIGHT WITH A BROKEN EYE SOCKET

A fighter once **had his eye socket shattered mid-fight—but still won!**

At **UFC 199 in 2016,** Michael Bisping challenged Luke Rockhold for the middleweight title. Early in the fight, **Rockhold landed a hard punch that fractured Bisping's orbital bone, causing his eye to swell rapidly.**

Despite the painful injury and impaired vision, **Bisping kept pressing forward and shocked the world by knocking Rockhold out in the first round to become the UFC champion!** Winning a world title with a broken eye socket? That's legendary toughness.

Mind-Blowing MMA Fact #94

MIND-BLOWING MMA FACT #94

THE ONLY UFC FIGHTER TO WIN AFTER GETTING KNOCKED DOWN FOUR TIMES

A fighter once **got dropped four times in a single fight—but still came back to win!**

At **UFC 236 in 2019**, Dustin Poirier and Max Holloway fought for the interim lightweight title in a high-paced war. Poirier **knocked Holloway down four times** with powerful punches, but Holloway refused to quit.

Despite being rocked multiple times, **Holloway kept pushing forward, landed over 200 strikes, and took Poirier to the final bell.** Poirier won by unanimous decision, but Holloway's resilience made it one of the greatest fights in UFC history!

Mind-Blowing MMA Fact #95

THE ONLY UFC FIGHTER TO WIN A FIGHT WHILE BARELY ABLE TO WALK

A fighter once **had his legs completely shut down—but still won!**

At **UFC 252 in 2020**, Sean O'Malley faced Marlon Vera in a highly anticipated bantamweight clash. Early in the fight, **Vera landed a calf kick that damaged O'Malley's peroneal nerve**, causing his leg to give out completely.

Despite barely being able to stand, **O'Malley continued to fight, hopping on one leg and throwing strikes.** However, Vera capitalized on the injury and won by TKO. Though he lost, **O'Malley's heart and determination to keep going were unforgettable.**

Mind-Blowing MMA Fact #96

MIND-BLOWING MMA FACT #96

THE FIGHTER WHO WON A UFC FIGHT WITH A BROKEN ANKLE

A fighter once **broke his ankle mid-fight—but still fought through the pain and won!**

At **UFC Fight Night 150 in 2019,** Mike Perry faced Alex Oliveira in a welterweight war. Early in the fight, **Perry suffered a fractured ankle while checking a kick.**

Despite the severe injury, **he kept throwing bombs, landing takedowns, and pushing forward for three full rounds.** He won by unanimous decision, later revealing that he had fought most of the bout **with a broken ankle!**

Mind-Blowing MMA Fact #97

MIND-BLOWING MMA FACT #97

THE FIGHTER WHO WON A UFC FIGHT WITH A BROKEN FOREARM

A fighter once **blocked a kick, broke his forearm**—but still won the fight!

At **UFC 221 in 2018,** Yoel Romero faced Luke Rockhold in a crucial middleweight fight. Early in the bout, **Romero blocked a powerful head kick, instantly fracturing his forearm.**

Despite the painful injury, **Romero kept throwing punches and landed a brutal knockout in the third round!** Fighting with a broken forearm and still scoring a KO? That's terrifying power!

Mind-Blowing MMA Fact #98

THE FIGHTER WHO WON A UFC FIGHT AFTER LOSING A PINT OF BLOOD

A fighter once **lost so much blood mid-fight that the canvas was drenched—but still won!**

At **UFC Fight Night 81 in 2016**, Eddie Alvarez faced Anthony Pettis in a grueling lightweight battle. Early in the fight, **Alvarez suffered a deep cut on his forehead**, causing him to bleed heavily throughout the fight.

Despite **losing nearly a pint of blood**, Alvarez pushed forward, controlled the grappling exchanges, and **won by split decision!** After the fight, doctors confirmed that Alvarez had bled so much that he required multiple stitches and IV fluids.

Mind-Blowing MMA Fact #99

THE ONLY FIGHTER TO WIN WITH A COMPLETELY SWOLLEN SHUT EYE

A fighter once **fought an entire round completely blind in one eye—and still won!**

At **UFC 136 in 2011**, Frankie Edgar defended his lightweight title against Gray Maynard in a brutal five-round war. Early in the fight, **Maynard landed a massive punch that caused Edgar's eye to swell completely shut.**

Despite barely being able to see, **Edgar made an incredible comeback, knocked Maynard down multiple times, and finished him by TKO in the fourth round!** Winning a championship fight with one functional eye? That's legendary heart.

Mind-Blowing MMA Fact #100

THE ONLY UFC FIGHTER TO WIN A FIGHT WITH A COMPLETELY BROKEN JAW

A fighter once **broke his jaw in the first round—but still fought to victory!**

At **UFC 201 in 2016,** Tyron Woodley challenged Robbie Lawler for the welterweight title. Early in the fight, **Lawler suffered a broken jaw from a devastating right hand.**

Despite the severe injury, **he kept fighting, absorbing more punishment, and refusing to quit.** However, Woodley's power was too much, and he finished Lawler by knockout in the first round to claim the title.

Fighting through a completely broken jaw? That's championship-level grit!

CONCLUSION

Congratulations! You've just battled through *100 Mind-Blowing MMA Facts* and explored the wild, unpredictable world of mixed martial arts. From unbelievable knockouts to fighters overcoming the impossible, this book has shown that **MMA is more than just a sport—it's a spectacle of heart, grit, and absolute chaos.**

But here's the thing about MMA—it's always evolving. For every incredible moment you've read, **there are countless more yet to unfold.** Maybe this book has deepened your appreciation for the sport, or perhaps it's opened your eyes to the sheer madness that happens inside (and sometimes outside) the Octagon.

One thing's for sure: **MMA will never stop delivering jaw-dropping moments.** Whether you're a fighter, a fan, or just someone who loves a good underdog story, there will always be more **shocking knockouts, historic come-**

backs, and mind-blowing feats of toughness waiting in the cage.

So as you close this book, remember—**this isn't the end of the story.** The next great MMA moment is just one fight away.

Until next time, stay fearless, stay curious, and **keep your guard up—because in MMA, anything can happen.**

ACKNOWLEDGEMENTS

Creating *100 Mind-Blowing MMA Facts* has been a journey filled with passion, late-night fight replays, and a deep appreciation for the warriors who step into the Octagon. While my name is on the cover, this book wouldn't exist without the inspiration, support, and energy from some truly incredible people.

First, a huge thank you to **the fighters**—past, present, and future—who put it all on the line every time they step into the cage. Your heart, resilience, and sheer toughness have created **some of the most unforgettable moments in sports history.** This book is a celebration of your legendary feats.

To my **family and friends**, who patiently endured my endless discussions about knockouts, submissions, and the craziest moments in MMA—you're the real MVPs. Your encouragement (and ability to tolerate my enthusiasm) kept me going through every page.

To **the MMA fans**—whether you've been watching since the early days of no-holds-barred fighting or just discovered the sport, **this book is for you.** Your passion for the fights, the fighters, and the unpredictable madness of MMA is what keeps this sport growing and evolving.

And finally, to **MMA itself**—thank you for being the most thrilling, unpredictable, and mind-blowing sport on the planet. You've given us stories of grit, glory, and absolute chaos, and I'm grateful to share just a few of them.

Here's to MMA, to the warriors who make it great, and to the next fight that will leave us speechless.

ABOUT THE AUTHOR

Felix Grayson is a storyteller at heart, driven by an insatiable curiosity for the **strange, surprising, and downright unpredictable moments in sports.** With a passion for uncovering the wildest and most unbelievable tales from the world of **MMA**, Felix has crafted *100 Mind-Blowing MMA Facts* to entertain, amaze, and spark wonder in fight fans of all ages.

When he's not digging through archives or chasing down the next jaw-dropping MMA moment, Felix enjoys **watching classic fights, breaking down legendary knockouts, and debating GOAT rankings over a cold drink.** A firm believer in the magic of combat sports and the power of a good story, Felix invites you to take this journey through **MMA's most unpredictable moments**, proving that inside the cage, **anything can happen.**

www.ingramcontent.com/pod-product-compliance
Lightning Source LLC
Chambersburg PA
CBHW030318080526
44584CB00012B/617